NOSE

HUMAN BODY

Robert James

The Rourke Press, Inc.
Vero Beach, Florida 32964

PHOTO CREDITS
All photos © Kyle Carter except page 21 © Frank Balthis

Library of Congress Cataloging-in-Publication Data

James, Robert, 1942-
    The nose / by Robert James.
        p. cm. — (Human body)
    Includes index.
    Summary: Describes the anatomy of the human nose, explains
how to protect the nose and care for a nosebleed, and includes
information on other animal noses.
    ISBN 1-57103-101-4
    1. Nose—Anatomy—Juvenile literature.   [1. Nose.]
I. Title II. Series: James, Robert, 1942- Human body
QM505.J36   1995
611'.86—dc20   95–4637
                                                                          CIP
                                                                          AC

Printed in the USA

TABLE OF CONTENTS

THE NOSE

Your nose is more than just the part of your face that would be the first to bump a door.

Your nose helps to tell you when bacon is frying and orange blossoms are in bloom. Your nose warns you when smoke is in the air. Your nose picks up the fresh scent of cookies and the not-so-fresh scent of spoiled milk.

Your nose, though, is more than a receiver of smells. It is a built-in air conditioner and filter.

Your nose picks up smells in the air and transfers them to your brain   5

THE OUTER NOSE

Your nose is shaped by bones and **cartilage** (KART el idj). Cartilage is tough, but it's not as hard or stiff as bone.

Everyone's nose has a different shape. Each nose, whatever its shape, works the same.

The two holes at the tip of the nose are nostrils. They are the openings to airways that lead into your head and lungs.

Nostrils in the nose, separated by the septum, are the beginnings of airways to the lungs

INSIDE THE NOSE

The **nasal** (NAY zul), or nose, pathways are wet with **mucus** (MUKE us). Mucus is as sticky as honey. It works with nasal hairs to collect dust.

Each breath you take draws millions of tiny, unseen particles into your nose—and lungs. Some of the particles are dust and germs. Your nose traps many of the dust and germ particles before they reach your throat and lungs.

While your nose is cleaning the air, it's also warming it.

A sneeze blows out mucus and some of the dust and germs trapped inside the nose

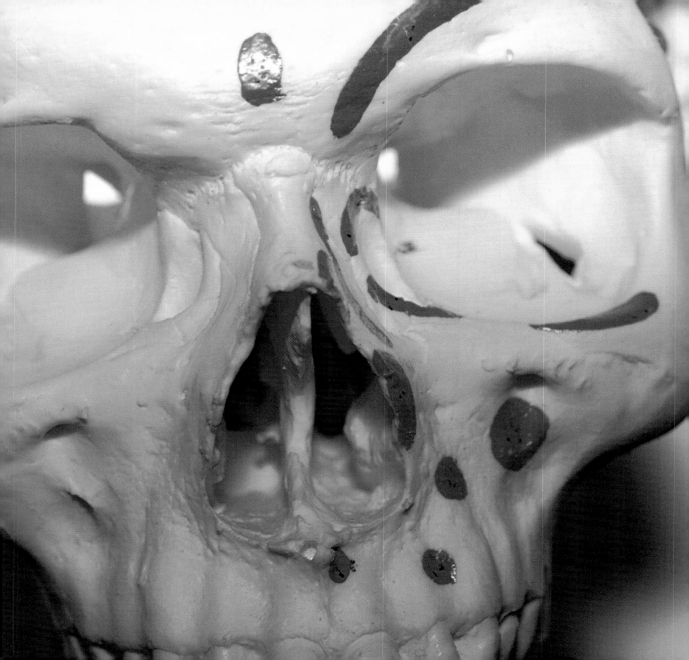

SINUSES

The nose **cavity** (KAH vih tee), or hollow, inside the skull connects to four groups of sinuses. Each sinus is also a cavity.

Sinuses surround the nose in the front part of the skull. They contain air and mucus. Sinuses help to warm and moisten the fresh air we breathe.

Like the nose itself, sinuses help clean air by filtering dust. If the sinus is infected with germs, mucus drains into the nose.

A model of a human skull shows the
nasal opening in the center of the skull

The nose is a great landing pad for a butterfly

The elephant's nose helps it take a shower, dust bath, or mouthful of leaves

ODORS

Your nose and brain work together to give you a sense of smell. The sense of smell turns on when an odor, or smell, is released into the air.

Odors come from tiny particles called **molecules** (MAHL uh kyoulz). We can't see molecules, but they are in the air. Our noses tell us that!

Noses sometimes carry strong,
unpleasant odors, or smells

NOSE AND BRAIN

Nerves (NERVZ) are tiny feelers in our flesh. The nerves in nasal passages are sensitive to odors.

The nerves send an odor message to the brain. The brain receives the message and instantly lets us know what we're smelling.

The sense of smell helps our sense of taste. People whose noses are plugged lose much of their ability to taste.

The human sense of taste works together with the sense of smell

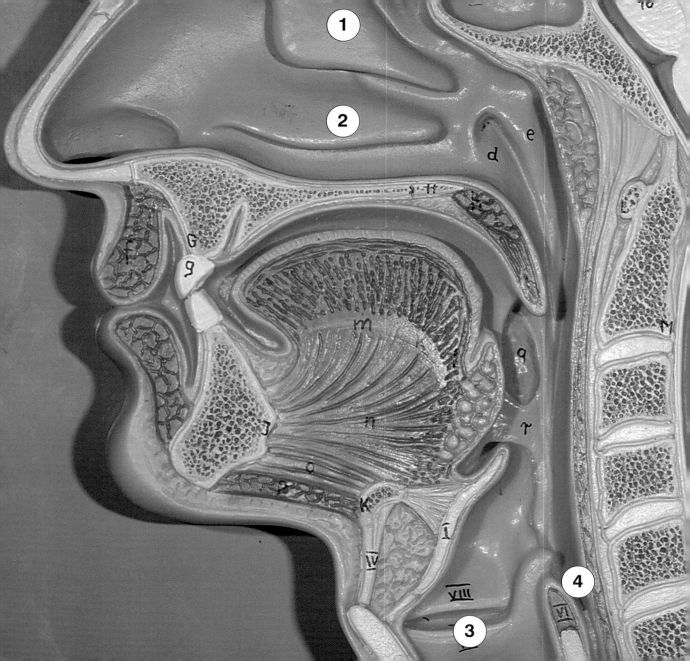

NOSE AND THROAT

You can breathe through your nose or mouth. Both the nose airway and the mouth connect to your "breathing tubes."

That main tube is the **trachea** (TRAY kee uh), an airway that leads from the lungs in our chest. The trachea and other connected airways pass through our throat and to the nose and mouth.

1. One of the sinuses
2. Nasal airway passage
3. Trachea and other airways
4. Esophagus

PROTECTING THE NOSE

Because it sticks out, the nose takes more than its share of "hits." Football players protect their noses with a nose or face guard on their helmets. Most people, however, just try to keep their noses out of trouble. Still, bloody and broken noses are common.

You can usually stop a nosebleed within a few minutes. Sit with your chin on your chest and pinch your nostrils together.

Dirt bikers protect their noses with strong, wraparound helmets

ANIMAL NOSES

Many animals have strange-looking noses. The longest and largest belongs to the elephant. The elephant uses its nose, or trunk, to gather food and water as well as for many other purposes.

One of the keenest senses of smell belongs to the bear. Bears and many other four-legged animals, such as wolves and dogs, have much sharper senses of smell than people.

Glossary

cartilage (KART el idj) — strong, flexible body tissue found in the outer ear and nose

cavity (KAH vih tee) — a hollowed out place, a shallow hole

molecules (MAHL uh kyoulz) — particles too small to be seen

mucus (MUKE us) — a slimy liquid produced by the skin linings inside the nose and elsewhere

nasal (NAY zul) — referring to the nose and its airways

nerves (NERVZ) — the sensitive "feelers" in flesh that send messages to the brain

trachea (TRAY kee uh) — the major tube for the passage of air to the lungs

INDEX